Stories of
JESUS

Illustrated by Patricia Ludlow
Retold and designed by Desmond Marwood

Brown Watson

ENGLAND

CONTENTS

THE BIRTH OF JESUS

About two thousand years ago, God sent the angel Gabriel to visit Mary, a young maiden who lived in Nazareth in the land of Galilee. She was getting ready for her marriage to a carpenter named Joseph. Gabriel told Mary that God had chosen her to bear His son and that the baby's name was to be Jesus. "The child shall be Holy," Gabriel told Mary, "and shall be called the Son of God. There shall be no end to His Kingdom." Mary married Joseph and they continued to live in Nazareth. At that time, it was the law that everyone must go back to their home town to register for payment of taxes. So, even though Jesus was soon to be born, Mary had to set off with Joseph on the long journey to Bethlehem, in the land of Judea. Bethlehem was crowded with people and there was no room for them at the inn. Joseph and Mary could find shelter only in a stable and that was where Jesus was born. Mary wrapped baby Jesus warmly and placed him in a manger for a crib. Outside Bethlehem, shepherds were alarmed by a bright light in the sky and the appearance of an angel. The angel told them that a Saviour called Christ the Lord had been born and that he was lying in a manger in Bethlehem. The shepherds hurried off to see this child who was the Son of God. Later, Wise Men from the east arrived with gifts of gold, frankincense and myrrh. When Herod, King of Judea, heard about the birth of Jesus, the Son of God, he feared he may grow up to be a rival leader and ordered the deaths of all new babies born in Bethlehem.

THE BOYHOOD OF JESUS

To escape the cruelty of King Herod, Joseph and Mary fled with baby Jesus from Judea to the safety of Egypt. They lived there for two years until news of King Herod's death made it possible for them to return in safety to Nazareth, where their home still remained at the back of Joseph's workshop. There, Jesus was able to grow up, enjoying the village life of Nazareth.

Jesus joined in games with the other children. He listened to the storytellers and spent happy boyhood years.

When Jesus became twelve years of age he celebrated what was, and still is, a special birthday for all Jewish boys. It was a 'coming of age', something like our own twenty-first birthday celebrations of today. From then on, Jesus would be treated almost as though he had become a man. He had to learn a trade, so he chose to follow in Joseph's footsteps and become a carpenter.

Jesus was now old enough to join with the elders and other young people on their annual pilgrimage to the Feast of the Passover in Jerusalem. Earlier, Jesus had been able only to watch as others made preparations for the eighty-mile journey to Jerusalem. Everything needed for a week's walking and camping in the open air was loaded onto carts drawn by mules, until at last the long caravan of pilgrims was ready to set out for Jerusalem. Now Jesus was a young man and old enough to join the excitement. For the first time, he would see Jerusalem and take part in the Feast of the Passover.

The party of pilgrims from Nazareth stayed in Jerusalem for a few days and then set off back home. Joseph and Mary did not see Jesus on the first day of the homeward journey and thought he must be with his friends. When he was nowhere to be found among the caravan of travellers on the second day, they realised he must have stayed behind in Jerusalem. They had left without him.

Joseph and Mary went back to Jerusalem and for three days searched the city in vain for news of Jesus. Then, Mary could scarcely believe her eyes when they found him in the Temple. He was surrounded by scholars and wise men, listening to their talk and joining in their discussions. The elders were amazed that such a young boy could understand so much about life and could speak so wisely on such matters.

Such praise did not stop Joseph and Mary from being cross with Jesus for not having told them he wanted to stay on in Jerusalem. They were even more annoyed that Jesus, a young boy, had gone into such an important place as the Temple. "We have searched for you for three days," Mary scolded him, "and we were tired and worried!"

"Why did you need to search for me?" Jesus asked them. "Did you not know that I must be about my Father's business?"

Joseph and Mary were puzzled by these words, for surely Joseph was the father of Jesus and a carpenter had no business in the Temple. They did not understand that when Jesus said "my Father's business" he meant God's work.

JOHN THE BAPTIST

John the Baptist was a holy man who lived in the land of Galilee. He was born the son of his father Zacharias and mother Elizabeth. They were two elderly people thought to be past the age at which they could have children. But, as happened some months later to Mary, when she was chosen to be the mother of Jesus, God sent the angel Gabriel to them with a special message. Gabriel told Zacharias that Elizabeth would have a son and the child would become a messenger for God. So the son, named John, was born a few months before the birth of Jesus. From childhood, John was devoted to God's service. He led a simple life, ate plain food and avoided strong drinks. He wore simple clothes and lived mostly in the desert. His standards in all things were high. He was very strict and quick to correct people about any misbehaviour. People crowded to his meetings at which he gave lessons on good and proper ways to behave. Many even wondered if he was the Son of God. He denied this and promised that one day, someone who was the Saviour, would come amongst them.

The day came when Jesus, who by then was about thirty years old, went into the desert and joined the crowd of people waiting to be baptised by John. The moment John saw Jesus he knew who he was and asked why he was to baptise him. "Surely, it is you who should be

6

baptising me," said John. Jesus explained it was God's wish that John should baptise him. Later, as Jesus arose from the water of baptism, the Spirit of God came down upon him from Heaven above and a voice from above said: "This is my beloved Son, in whom I am well pleased."

With his mind full of God his Father, Jesus went out into the wilderness for forty days and forty nights. He wished only to be alone and able to think. He ate nothing and as he became weak the Devil came to him and promised him anything in the world if only he would give up doing God's work.

The Devil challenged him to show he had powers which would prove to him that he was the Son of God, such as changing stones into bread or throwing himself from a high temple and landing unhurt.

"Get thee behind me, Satan," Jesus told the Devil, "for it is written 'You shall worship the Lord thy God and only Him shall you serve!'"

Jesus did not give in to the Devil's temptations and went back to Galilee strengthened to carry on with the work of God.

Meanwhile, John the Baptist carried on with his work for God. Time and again John told the people of King Herod's wickedness in breaking God's laws. Finally, exasperated by these attacks upon him, the King had John shut away in prison and later executed.

THE MARRIAGE FEAST

Jesus and some friends, along with his mother Mary, were invited to a marriage feast one day. It was a big wedding with many guests and before long all the wine had been drunk. Mary told Jesus what had happened and she called the servants over to join them.

Jesus told the servants to fill six large stone water pots with water. Mary urged them to do as Jesus asked and the pots were filled to their brims with water.

Then, Jesus told the servants to pour drinks from the pots and serve them to the master in charge of the wedding feast. The master was truly amazed when he tasted the drinks, because the water had been changed into wine. He just didn't know what was happening, but the servants did – a miracle had been performed!

This first miracle of Jesus proved his power and resulted in many confirming their belief in him.

THE BLIND MAN

Jesus was visiting the town of Bethsaida when the friends and relatives of a blind person brought him to Jesus and asked him to heal the man. Jesus took the man by the hand and led him out of the town. When they were alone, Jesus put some spittle from his own mouth onto the man's eyes and placed his hands over the man's eyes. Then, he took his hands away and asked the man if he could see anything.

The man said he could see men looking like trees and moving about. Again, Jesus covered the man's eyes with his hands. When he removed them this time, the man looked up and said he now saw everything clearly. His sight had come back to him. Jesus sent the man home with orders to tell no one what had happened or how his eyes had been made to see again.

THE FIRST DISCIPLES

The first people Jesus tried to teach were those who lived in his home village of Nazareth, but they did not take much notice of him. They had known Jesus all his life, simply as the son of Joseph the carpenter. They found it hard to believe that he who had been "the boy next door" could now tell them what they should or should not do with their lives.

This made Jesus decide to leave Nazareth and visit Capernaum and other cities in Galilee where people did listen to what he had to say. In fact, huge crowds followed him as he preached, healed the sick and cast out devils.

One day, on the shore of Lake Gennesaret, Jesus asked a fisherman named Simon if he could stand on his boat to preach to the crowd gathered on the shore. Simon agreed and he and his brother Andrew moved the boat a short distance from the shore so that more people could get a better view of Jesus and hear more clearly what he had to say.

When he finished preaching, Jesus asked Simon and Andrew to go further out into deep water and start to fish. Although Simon and Andrew had fished all night and caught nothing, they did as Jesus asked and dropped their nets into the water. In no time at all they had caught so many fish that their boat almost sank. They called for their friend James to come and help and soon his boat also was filled to overflowing.

Simon knew then that Jesus had powers he did not understand and it was with some fear that he knelt before him. James and Andrew were also afraid. They asked Jesus to leave them alone, but he urged all three fishermen not to be afraid, telling them that in future they would become fishers of men, not fish.

So when they came ashore, Simon, Andrew and James left everything behind them to become followers of Jesus. They were his first disciples, as they are called. Gradually, Jesus gathered nine more disciples around him. They were John, Philip, Thomas, Bartholomew, Matthew, James, Simon called Zelotes, Judas the brother of James and Judas Escariot.

THE DAUGHTER OF JAIRUS

A man named Jairus knelt down before Jesus and pleaded with him to visit his home where his twelve-year-old daughter was very ill. Everyone felt that she was sure to die. So, Jesus agreed to go with Jairus, but so many people were gathered around them that getting through the crowd was slow and the journey was taking a long time.

Before they could reach the home of Jairus, a messenger arrived to tell the poor man that he was too late. His daughter was already dead and there was no need to trouble Jesus any further. Jesus told the grieving father not to be afraid, but to believe in Him and that all would be well.

When they arrived at the man's house, Jesus would allow only his followers Peter, James and John, along with the girl's parents, to enter with him into the room where the girl was on her bed.

The parents sobbed at the sight of the girl lying so white and still, but Jesus assured them their daughter was not dead. He said that she was only sleeping. Jesus took the girl by the hand and told her to sit up. The girl's soul came back into her body and she rose up from the bed and walked around the room.

Soon, the girl was so full of life that Jesus said she was in need of something to eat. Then he left the house, ordering her parents to say nothing to anyone of what had happened.

THE CRIPPLED BEGGAR

There was a pool which everyone said had miraculous powers because after the waters moved, then calmed, the first person to be immersed in it would be healed. Beside this pool lay a poor beggar who had been crippled for many years. He was unable to stand or walk. Sadly, the man had no friends and although he asked passers-by to lift him into the pool in the hope that his limbs might become strong again, they all refused to help. Jesus was out walking one Sabbath day when he came upon the beggar lying beside the pool upon his bed of blankets. He stopped and listened to the man's story and offered to help.

Jesus simply told the beggar to pick up his bed and walk. Instantly, it seemed to the beggar that his arms and legs became strong again. Amazed, he rose to stand upon his feet. The beggar thanked Jesus, before picking up his bed and belongings and carrying them away.

Later, the enemies of Jesus questioned the beggar about what had happened. They claimed that on the Sabbath day, nobody should do anything but pray. It was not right to do anything else, such as carrying bedding. When they learned Jesus had ordered the man to do this they were even more annoyed with him.

FEEDING OF THE FIVE THOUSAND

Travelling throughout the land with his disciples, Jesus became so famous for preaching and healing the sick that many believed he might be John the Baptist who had been born again. Although King Herod didn't really believe this, he very much wanted to meet Jesus. He wanted to know if Jesus was preaching about things which were going to cause him any trouble ruling over his subjects, as John the Baptist had done.

That was why, when Jesus heard that King Herod's soldiers were searching for him, he led his disciples to a lonely place in the desert near the city of Bethsaida.

It was a place where Jesus was sure no one would look for him. However, his followers somehow found out where it was and huge crowds came to hear him preach and to be healed by him.

Jesus met with his followers and, as many hours went by, the disciples became hungry. They knew that all the people must be hungry also, but in the desert there was nothing to eat and nowhere to buy food. When they suggested to Jesus that he should send the people away, back to their homes, he simply told his disciples to give the people something to eat. He asked that they put before him any food they had brought with them for their own use on their journey.

A boy who was in the crowd had only five loaves of bread and two fishes. The disciples reminded Jesus there were at least five thousand people in the crowd of followers. They could not understand how it would be possible for so many to be fed with such a small amount of food.

Jesus asked for the crowd to sit down in groups of fifty people. He then took the five loaves and two fishes and blessed them before breaking them all into pieces. He put the pieces into baskets and told the disciples to share out the pieces among the people. To everyone's astonishment, the more they shared out the food, the more there seemed to be in their baskets. Everyone ate as much as they wanted and at the end of the meal there still remained twelve baskets of left-overs to be collected.

The five thousand had been fed by a miracle!

JESUS WALKS ON WATER

After feeding his five thousand followers, Jesus sent the crowds away. Later the same day, he asked his disciples to get into a boat and go ahead of him across the water to Gennesaret. Jesus stayed behind, so that he could go alone into the mountains and pray.

The disciples were still in their boat on the water when evening came. A strong wind was blowing up, making such heavy waves that the disciples were afraid their boat might sink. They became even more afraid when they saw the figure of a man walking towards them over the water. They thought it must be a ghost!

As the figure got nearer to them it looked like Jesus, but they could not believe their eyes and screamed out in fear. But it was Jesus and he called out to them not to be afraid. He told them to be calm.

Even then, the disciples were not sure it was Jesus walking on the water towards them. Peter shouted: "If it really is you, help me to walk on water as well." Jesus simply replied: "Come!"

The other disciples watched as Peter climbed over the side of the boat and stepped onto the water. At first, he did walk safely on the waves towards Jesus, but then he became frightened by the howling wind. Startled, he looked down at his feet and called to Jesus for help as he began to sink. Jesus reached out his hand to catch hold of Peter and lifted him up again. Jesus explained that Peter had sunk into the water because he had shown such little faith in him. "Why did you doubt me?" Jesus asked Peter.

Jesus helped Peter towards the boat and they both stepped on board. After that, the disciples believed firmly that Jesus was indeed the Son of God and that if their faith remained strong, they were able to do anything they chose.

RESPECTABLE OR REPENTANT

A Pharisee who, along with his friends, praised God and His work, had so far been unable to properly understand Jesus. They were not quite sure what to make of him. So, one evening, the Pharisee called his friends together and invited Jesus to join them for supper, in order that they might talk and learn more about him.

During the meal, a woman entered the room. She was weeping and threw herself down before Jesus. Sobbing, the woman asked Jesus to forgive her for all her past sins. As she spoke, her tears fell upon his feet and she dried them with her hair. Then, she rubbed the feet of Jesus with a soothing ointment. She had brought the ointment with her, knowing the feet of Jesus would be sore after the many miles he had walked on his travels.

While she did this, the Pharisee only sneered at the woman, for he knew that she had not led a good life. But Jesus scolded him for speaking to her in that manner. He pointed out that while the Pharisee had only invited him to supper to pry into his life, to ask questions and find out all about him, the weeping woman had come because she wanted to be forgiven for her sins. For that, Jesus told the Pharisee and his friends, the woman meant more to him than all of them. "I forgive you!" Jesus told the woman.

JESUS IS ASKED FOR HELP

Decapolis was only a small country, so news of the arrival of Jesus spread quickly throughout the land. Many people soon knew that he was amongst them. Before long, Jesus and his disciples were surrounded by a large crowd of country folk who had brought with them a man. He had been deaf and almost dumb since he was born.

The man's friends asked Jesus if there was anything he could do to cure the man's deafness and also make him able to speak.

Jesus took the man to a quiet place, away from the crowds that had been attracted by his presence in the land.

When they were alone, he placed his hands gently on the man's ears and touched his tongue with spittle.

Then, Jesus looked up to Heaven and said: "Be opened!"

The man looked up at Jesus in astonishment. For the first time in his life he could hear. He opened his mouth and mumbled his first few words.

Yes, he could also speak! Jesus said he should not tell about what had happened. Overjoyed the man ran off to show his friends that now he was able to hear and speak.

THE CENTURION'S SERVANT

In the time when Jesus lived, there were few doctors and people often suffered for years without any proper help or treatment for their illnesses or disabilities. So, when they heard that Jesus was able to cure sicknesses, large crowds began to follow him about.

Jesus was on his way to Capernaum when he was spoken to by a centurion, an officer in the Roman army that ruled the land.

The centurion told Jesus that one of his servants was ill and in pain. Jesus offered to go to the centurion's home to cure the man, but the centurion would not even consider that idea. He told Jesus that he did not feel himself to be important enough for such special treatment. It would be good enough for Jesus simply to say the word there and then for his servant to be cured, and he knew that would be sufficient to make the man well again. There was no need for Jesus to go to the bother of visiting his home to see the sick man.

"I am used to giving orders," the centurion told Jesus. "I understand these things. If I say to my soldiers 'Go!' they go and if I say 'Come!' they come. Please, just give a word of command for my servant to be made well. I am not worthy for you to do more."

It was unusual for an important centurion to speak in such a humble manner or to show such respect for others. Onlookers were surprised, while Jesus told his followers that he had never before seen such faith as was shown by the centurion. So, Jesus told the centurion to go on his way, assuring him that his servant would be cured without the need for him to see the man. Sure enough, within the hour, the centurion's servant was healed and feeling well again.

THE SOWING OF SEEDS

Jesus often told stories to the crowds who gathered to hear him preach, so they could more easily understand what he was explaining to them about life and the proper way to live. These teaching stories were called parables.

One story was about a farmer sowing seeds, scattering them as he walked through the fields. Some of the seeds thrown by the farmer landed on the roadside where they were trodden down and eaten by the birds. Some fell on rocky ground, but soon withered because the ground was dry. Some seeds fell among thorn bushes, where they grew at first until the bushes became so thick they choked them.

But, some seeds fell on good ground where they grew well and produced a fine crop.

Then, Jesus said that only a few people would be able to understand the meaning of the story. The disciples said they couldn't understand it at all, so Jesus explained to them that the seeds were meant to be the words or teachings of God. Words that fell by the roadside were heard, but by people who ignored them.

Those that fell on rocky ground were the words heard by people who listened to God. Those people were good for a while, but then forgot and went back to their bad old ways of living.

The seeds that fell among thorns were the words heard by people who meant well and tried to be good, but were always so busy with work or having fun that they had no time for anything else. Those seeds that fell on good ground were the words heard by people who remembered them and always tried to obey God's rules.

MORE JOY IN HEAVEN

The Pharisees and scribes thought it was wrong for Jesus to speak with some types of people who were among the crowds that always came to hear what he had to tell them. They complained that Jesus had received sinners and mixed with them too freely. So, to reprove the Pharisees and scribes, Jesus told them the story of the man who owned a flock of a hundred sheep. One day the man counted his sheep and was alarmed to discover that one must have wandered away and was missing. Immediately, the man left his other ninety-nine sheep grazing together in safety and set off to find his one lost sheep.

After a long search in the wilderness, the man found his lost sheep. He placed the tired animal across his shoulders and carried it home to put it back into the flock.

Then, he rejoiced with his friends to celebrate the finding of his one lost sheep.

Jesus explained that in the same way, there is more joy in Heaven over one sinner that repents than the niney-nine who have no need to repent.

THE GOOD SAMARITAN

A lawyer asked Jesus how he could make sure of getting to Heaven and Jesus told him that he should love God and also love his neighbour as himself. When the lawyer asked who was his neighbour, Jesus replied by telling the story of the good Samaritan.

The story was about a certain man who was a Jew. He was travelling from Jersualem to Jericho when he was attacked and robbed by thieves. They beat him, took all that he had and left him for dead.

Later, a priest walked by and when he saw the injured man he passed by on the other side of the road.

Then came another man, called a Levite, and he too hurried by.

Next came a Samaritan and when he saw the injured man he felt sorry for him. He soothed the man's wounds with oil and bandaged them. The Samaritan put the injured man on his own horse and took him to an inn. There, he gave the innkeeper money and told him to care for the injured man. Before leaving, the Samaritan promised the innkeeper he would call in on his return journey and repay him if any more money was needed.

The good Samaritan man did this great act of care and kindness, even though the Jews and the Samaritans were known to hate each other.

Jesus then asked the lawyer whether the priest, the Levite or the Samaritan was the neighbour of the man who had been attacked by thieves The lawyer replied he thought that the Samaritan was the neighbour because he had been so kind to the injured man. Jesus told the lawyer he was correct and that he also should behave in that way to everyone he met in life.

THE MAN WHO KNOCKED

One time, the disciples asked Jesus how they should pray and he told them they should be like the man who knocked at the door of a friend's house very late at night. The man told his friend, who wasn't very happy at being woken from his sleep, that someone had come to stay with him at the end of a long journey. He had run out of bread and had no food to give to his visitor and wanted to borrow a loaf.

The friend inside the house called out to the man at the door to go away and not bother him. It was too late. He had already gone to bed and the house was locked up.

But the man at the door kept on knocking and knocking until his friend finally decided it was easier to get out of bed and give him the loaf, than trying to ignore him any longer.

Jesus told the disciples that in the same way as the man had kept knocking and knocking, so must they keep praying. "Ask and it shall be given to you," he told them. "Seek and you shall find."

THE FOOLISH MAIDENS

The followers of Jesus all hoped that one day they would go with him to Heaven. Jesus said they should always be prepared for whenever that day came. To help them understand what he meant, he told them the story of the ten maidens.

The ten maidens took their lamps with them in readiness for a special sort of wedding feast at which their job was to accompany the bridegroom into the feast. Five of the maidens were wise and took extra oil with them just in case it was needed to keep their lamps burning brightly. The other five were foolish and did not take any extra oil with them.

The bridegroom was so very late arriving that, by the time the maidens went outside to light his way into the feast, their lamps had gone out. The five wise maidens were able to use the extra oil they had brought with them to re-light their lamps. The foolish maidens, who hadn't brought any spare oil, had to rush away to the shops to buy more.

While the foolish maidens were away shopping, the five wise maidens had their lamps burning brightly and were able to light up the way for the bridegroom as they all went into the feast. The entrance door closed after them and when the foolish maidens returned it was still firmly shut. They were locked out from the feast they had so been looking forward to.

Jesus told his followers that this story showed how everyone should live wisely and always be prepared and ready for the day when God comes.

THE PRODIGAL SON

Jesus also told his followers the story of the man who had two sons. The younger son was an impatient young man. He couldn't wait for the part of the family fortune that he knew he would one day inherit, so he asked his father for his share to be paid straight away. The father did as his son asked and he was immediately given the money due to him.

The son packed his belongings, including the money, and left home to go and live in a far away country where he wasted his time and wealth on what he thought was having a good time. He lived recklessly and had very soon spent all his money. Then came a famine in the land in which he had settled. Food and shelter was hard to find and he had to live the life of a poor man.

After much searching, he got work with a farmer who sent him out into the fields to feed the pigs. He was so hungry that he even wanted to eat some of the pig food. The young man became really miserable. He remembered the comfort of the family home he'd left behind so long ago. There, even his father's servants had more than enough to eat.

That thought gave him the idea to set off back home and ask his father to take him in and give him a job as a servant.

The young man set off and when he at last arrived home he was in ragged clothes, tired and weak with hunger. Even so, his father was overjoyed to see him and welcomed him back with open arms. He ordered the servants to fetch his son the best robe, the finest jewelry and shoes for his feet. He also prepared a huge feast to celebrate his son's return.

Meanwhile, the elder son who was the brother of the son who had returned, had been hard at work as usual in his father's fields. He was making his way home and when he got near the house he could hear the sound of music and merrymaking. The servants told him it was the sound of his father's celebrations being held because his young brother had at last returned home. They told him about the feast of welcome his father had prepared.

The young man from the fields was very angry about the celebrations being held in honour of his brother and refused to go into the house. His father came out to plead with him, but the faithful son reminded him of the years he had worked for him in the fields without any reward that would have made it possible for him to have special celebrations or parties for his friends. Now, because the son who had wasted his wealth on reckless living had come back home, his father had even killed the fatted calf for a feast of celebration.

Gently, the father told his hard-working son that they were always close together and all that the father had was his. On the other hand, it was appropriate that they should all be glad about the return of his younger brother.

"He was lost and now he is found and therefore we should be glad," said the father.

PALM SUNDAY

It was almost time for the Feast of the Passover as Jesus and his disciples made their way towards Jerusalem. When they reached the hill known as the Mount of Olives, Jesus sent two disciples on ahead into Jerusalem. There, he told them, they would find a young ass, upon which no man had ever sat, tied up to a post. They were to release the animal and bring it back with them to Jesus.

If anyone asked why they were taking the animal, they were to reply: "Because the Lord has need of him."

The disciples soon returned with the ass and placed some of their clothes upon its back for Jesus to sit upon.

As Jesus rode upon the ass, the disciples spread more of their clothes before him onto the road. Huge crowds of people gathered as Jesus rode into the streets of Jerusalem. Many of them also cast down their clothes in front of him, while others cut down the leaves and branches of palm trees and spread them as a carpet on the road. Thousands bowed down before Jesus and cried aloud: "Blessed be the King who is coming in the name of the Lord!" So it was that Jesus was welcomed into Jerusalem.

Jesus was annoyed when he entered the city's Temple of God and found it was being used as a place for rascally moneylenders and those who sold doves, to do their business. He overturned their seats and tables and drove them out, telling the people that the Temple of God should be a house of prayer.

After that, Jesus and the people prayed in the Temple and the blind and the lame came to him there and he cured them.

However, the priests and the scribes were not pleased with Jesus and his work. The scribes were well educated and did the writing for the many who were themselves unable to write. Along with the priests, they had always been important and everyone looked up to them. Now, the

people talked about no-one but Jesus.
Also, they were embarrassed in front
of the people because Jesus won every
argument they tried to have with him.
The priests and the scribes were
also angry when they heard
the children in the Temple cry:
"Hosana to the son of David!" which
meant they thought Jesus was
descended from the great King David.
The priests asked Jesus if he could
hear what the children were saying
and he simply replied: "Out of the
mouths of babes and sucklings
come wise words."
All this made the priests and
scribes so furious that they
wanted to have Jesus killed,
but they dare not do so because
they were afraid this might cause
the crowds to rise up against them.

THE LAST SUPPER

The chief priests and scribes, along with the elders of the city of Jerusalem, did not give up discussing ways and means of arresting Jesus. They wished to take him swiftly and quietly, without causing any uproar among the people and it was a disciple of Jesus, named Judas Escariot, who made it possible for them to do this.

Judas Escariot, a very mean man, went secretly to the priests and agreed to betray Jesus to them. In return for payment to him of thirty pieces of silver, he promised to let the priests know of a time and place where they would be able to arrest Jesus quietly, without there being a crowd of people around him able to protest or defend him.

Meanwhile, the disciples were preparing the Feast of the Passover for Jesus and themselves. A man in Jerusalem had let them use a room in his house and in the evening Jesus and his twelve disciples sat down together at the long table. The disciples were sad because Jesus had told them he knew this would be the last

supper they would take together. He broke the bread, blessed it and handed it to the others. They drank the wine and passed it round amongst themselves.

After the supper, Jesus told his disciples that he knew one of them would betray him to the priests and elders of the city. He refused to tell which of them this would be, but he knew and whispered to Judas Escariot that what he had promised the priests he would do, he must go now and do quickly.

When Judas Escariot left the room, the other disciples thought Jesus had sent him to buy more things for the festival. They had no idea that he had gone to tell the whereabouts of Jesus to the priests of the city.

After Judas had left them, Jesus told his disciples that he would be with them only a little while longer. The disciples were puzzled when he said that where he was going they could not come, but they might be able to follow him later. Of course, Jesus meant that he would be with his Father in Heaven.

Their supper was finished and Jesus and the disciples left the city of Jerusalem and went to the Mount of Olives. There, he took them to a garden named Gethsemane and asked the disciples to rest

together while he went alone to pray at a place nearby. Three times he returned to find them all sleeping soundly.

Finally, Jesus woke the disciples and told them to go with him because he knew that the person who had betrayed his whereabouts to the priests was somewhere close by.

As Jesus spoke of this to his disciples, Judas Escariot stepped out from the bushes. With him were men sent by the priests and elders of Jerusalem, all armed with swords or clubs and ready to arrest Jesus.

Judas showed the men who amongst the gathering was Jesus, the one to be arrested, by going up to him, kissing him and saying: "Hail, Master!" Jesus was immediately arrested and taken before Pontius Pilate, the Roman governor. Pilate found nothing wrong with Jesus and washed his hands in front of the crowd to show he had nothing to do with punishing Jesus.

However, Jesus had offended too many important people who were determined to be rid of him. So, Jesus was killed upon a cross between two thieves suffering a similar punishment. Since then, for two thousand years, millions of people all over the world have believed that Jesus was truly the Son of God.